Without Protection

Gala Mukomolova

COFFEE HOUSE PRESS
Minneapolis

2019

Coffee House Press books are available to the trade through our primary distributor, Consortium Book Sales & Distribution, cbsd.com or (800) 283-3572. For personal orders, catalogs, or other information, write to info@coffeehousepress.org.

Coffee House Press is a nonprofit literary publishing house. Support from private foundations, corporate giving programs, government programs, and generous individuals helps make the publication of our books possible. We gratefully acknowledge their support in detail in the back of this book.

LIBRARY OF CONGRESS CATALOGING-IN-PUBLICATION DATA

Names: Mukomolova, Gala, author.
Title: Without protection / Gala Mukomolova.
Description: Minneapolis : Coffee House Press, 2019.
Identifiers: LCCN 2018040453 (print) | LCCN 2018043898 (ebook) |
    ISBN 9781566895521 | ISBN 9781566895439 (trade pbk.)
Classification: LCC PS3613.U395 (ebook) | LCC PS3613.U395 A6 2019
    (print) | DDC 811/.6—dc23
LC record available at https://lccn.loc.gov/2018040453

PRINTED IN THE UNITED STATES OF AMERICA

26 25 24 23 22 21 20 19   1 2 3 4 5 6 7 8

For all my relations, especially my father, who walked me toward this book and will never set a living eye upon it

Herein:

The Heroine & the Witch

Пойди туда, не знаю куда, принеси то, не знаю что
Go there—I know not where. Bring back—I know not what.

> *Vasilyssa, a maiden undone by the world, braves Baba Yaga's forest.
> Through the birch and underbrush she sees smoke, fence made of
> skulls, cat gnawing its own bone. There, a house spins on chicken legs.
> Living house, haunting.*

> *Vasilyssa sings a song she did not know was known to her and
> stills the house. "Do you come for your own sake or for the sake of
> another?" The house is Baba; transformed, terrible.*

> *Vasilyssa believes in truth, "I come in the name of others and I come
> in my own name. I come for fire and for you. All of this and some-
> thing else, something I've forgotten. Baba, I don't know why I come."*

> *The House regards her heroine. "You'll do."*

> *Vasilyssa at threshold, through.*

Without Protection

There's always a forest I know, little else
I was a child there was a forest
no one remembers

a meadow too, a field of wheat or
grass that stood dry and thin, waving
goodbye to me

My father took my hand
led me through it, I know
but when I close
my eyes the girl is alone in the field

Which berries are poisonous?
The girl knows very little
wants to be brave
says her name
bright like a bird might

calling a girl who lives
across the forest, a girl
with the same name, a friend

My first friend, the forest, creek running
down somewhere, wood swing wide
enough to hold us both

I know
which girl I was which girl was left
back in the old country, which is
only old to me

She gave me a birdcage for my bird, I think
I might have loved her a basket
full of beautiful poison berries

And the girl is not afraid of forests
or love's darkness; she drags an empty
cage into the forest no one sees

A poison branch, unknown to herself,
stroked and bent, come loose

Love made a clearing in the night where
a girl's will tamped down the grass
or: an eagerness

to claim and be claimed
I know the bird is dead, I feel it very near

Return

There are poets with history and poets without history, Tsvetaeva claimed, living through the ruin of Russia.

Karina says *disavow* every time I see her. We, the daughters between countries, wear our mean mothers like scarves around our necks.

Every visit, mine recounts all the wrongs done against her

ring sent for polishing returned with a lesser diamond, *Years of never rest and,* she looks at me, *nothing to be proud of.*

I am covered in welts and empty pockets so large sobs escape me in the back room of my landlord's fabric shop. He moves to wipe my tears

as if I'm his daughter or
I'm no one's daughter.

It's true, I let him take my hand, I am a girl who needs something. I slow cook bone grief, use a weak voice.

My mother calls me *the girl with holes in her hands* every time I lose something.

All Russian daughters were snowflakes once, and in their hair a ribbon long as their bodies, knotted and knotted and knotted into a large translucent bow.

It happens, teachers said, that a child between countries will refuse to speak. A girl with a hole in her throat, every day I opened the translation book.

Silent, I took my shoes off when I came home,
I put my house clothes on.

We had no songs, few rituals. On Yom Kippur, we lit a candle for the dead and no one knew a prayer.

We kept the candle lit, that's all.

The wave always returns, and always returns a different wave.
I was small. I built a self outside my self because a child needs shelter.

Not even you knew I was strange,
I ate the food my family ate, I answered to my name.

On the Brighton Beach boardwalk men sit in the rain shelters smelling of piss, shouting drunk genius into the afternoon sun. Men play chess on small portable sets, holding beach umbrellas for cover. Men take care of other men, raising them from wheelchairs and guiding them to benches and it looks just like slow dancing. So gentle. Someone has rolled blue carpets from the boards, over the beach, to the pale-blue water.

There are so many young mothers but my mother has hope for me too. She says *a beautiful girl like me, men must make advances all the time. A beautiful girl like me has to think of her future. A beautiful girl like me, well, cousin Lena turned forty and she quit that Los Angeles life and that Los Angeles girlfriend. Got herself a rich husband, an adopted baby. And, don't you know they love that baby? They love her despite how, in the wrong light, she's a little too brown.*

I'm furiously stuffing my mouth with black bread because this talk makes me angry and because I'm crying, staring down into my plate, thinking on last night—how you called me *difficult* when you could have called me *beautiful*. And here it is, *beautiful* tumbling out my mother's mouth like bad oil. More and more I imagine my dead body slumped beside me. It feels peaceful. *We're just having a heart-to-heart,* my mother says, *you shouldn't get so upset.*

We go around in a circle.
The back of a truck, one woman starts, *black sky too blurred for stars.*
Eight of us, the dark

> basement of a house; artists' retreat. We wade
> through beer bottles, sweat-soaked furniture.
> *What counts as the first time? Just the tip?*

Her cunt: blue bruise throbbing.
She turned away from me, would
not uncurl.

> Last night's party, tonight's party.
> What she remembers is what he told her.
> Another woman starts to cry and skips her turn.

I saw a woman lunge into the pit with no regard for gravity. She slammed a six-foot man to the ground, shattered his shoulder.

Marked by sweat and teenage rituals: lingering of strange tongues and beer fresh in my mouth like a punk song that has done its job. A woman weighs down the center of the B36 bus. Her face, something like a match struck in a thick night hallway, what fear is made of. When she speaks my name I am a swan slipping under a bridge, swallowed.

I was fifteen. I worked at a bagel place on Oriental Blvd. off Brighton Beach. It was summer and I had no idea who my friends were. I learned to juice pineapple and "refresh" a serving tub of cream cheese. I was a Bananarama song but all day the deli played "Piano Man." Russian businessmen tapped their pointed shoes and ordered shots of wheatgrass. I would call out to cold storage for cucumbers and Francisco would amble downstairs, swinging one between his legs, clicking his tongue.

Vasilyssa Comes to Call

Fuck. Baba's disembodied hand tracks her through
the thicket   branches snatch   blood on her dress.
Mud-kneed, Vasilyssa opens

Baba's gate.   Wide, the metal groans, an animal
nears: more teeth than dog.   Vasya's got no meat
                                         to please it.

One story with no mother's blessing: Baba rides her
mortar, pestle proud
                        against the bones and forest floor.
Behind her, a broom of birch that sweeps her traces.

♦

Vasilyssa always comes to call.   She's careful
with a name.   Twice is a song, three times a curse.

Which do you say in the mirror at night?   Which
one follows you down the street panting *come here
                        pretty girl, come here.*

♦

No firebird; ash is ash. Friday night fireworks break
the sky. Coney Island's all smoke; your eyes burn &

each blast thrums your bones. Never mind
                        the night walk, boardwalk planks lit
up from under with another life.

Come here, Красавица
                you know too much
                        you grow old too soon.

Body, mud-wet field

            Struck   one stone   one stone

home.

                        Who taught you to?

                        Who put you where they wanted you?

Once, I thwacked a ball far afield, uncatchable, white, hot as a sun

snaring my vision. The sky, each sock,
seared a pastry ridge into my shins

I ran.

                        Things don't fall apart. Things hold.

She calls me just like I knew she would. Two hours, twenty-four minutes is how long it takes her to shift from *never again* to *please, just come over*—I should know because it's the fourth time this week. No one's complaining, I'm seventeen, deep and deep in. She's in college, writing essays about *The Awakening.*

I'm up late deciphering Kate Chopin's angels for her because I'm a philosopher. She's got a primary my age and I don't think that's so weird if you don't. I pack for a slumber party and go to her place instead. She says *you don't have to . . . I mean . . . cunts can be really overwhelming up close.* I don't know what she means, fuck her for three hours 'cause she lets me.

She starts toward the bathroom, falls. *That's a weakness in the legs,* she instructs, *that's what you've done to me.* I leave her, 5 a.m., with a letter about the moon bouncing off her back. That's code for *I wish you'd face me.* She gets it and she doesn't.

Received

To: IIMermaidTearSII@aol.com
From: Skater-----@aol.com

Subject: hi

Body: look this over pleeeeease?

[abstract][italics mine]

Edna's idealism lends to her a virginal and innocent quality. Though she has experienced sexual initiation through being a mother, she has not experienced her sexuality. The awakening of her sexuality is strongly symbolized by her connection with the sea; it is almost as if her body is being drawn to its currents: "A feeling of exultation overtook her, as if some power of significant import had been given her to control the working of her body and soul. She grew daring and reckless, overestimating her strength. She wanted to swim far out, where no woman had swum before" (Chopin 73). Edna longed to be weighed down; she was yearning for the merging of her body and the ocean. When we ignore the body, we become more easily victimized by it; for Edna, her body became an explosion of revelation that she didn't know was attainable.

High school wasn't always two towers crashing. Girls sunned on cement blocks, a playground between housing projects on the Upper West Side. Our pinhole cameras reeled us in, time of exposure: five seconds, ten. In the darkroom, we were the light. Slaveya surfaced in her own image: lipstick Elvis incarnate, lush dark hair pulled back and pompadoured. I rode a stone whale, my crinoline skirt falling in a soft wave over its head.

What wasn't dangerous? We had all heard a woman ran in one side of Central Park and did not come out the other. Polish Mike liked to sit at the Juilliard squares, waiting. We'd come over and smoke. You didn't need to know his age; you didn't even need to pay him. My friend gave him head at my fifteenth birthday party. I don't remember what I saw. Some girl said he spent a lot of time on the swings, alone. That was supposed to redeem him.

Tenderness.   Once you read a book.

                                        It was called *Tenderness.*

A girl saw a sociopath smile on TV and knew

                    her tongue belonged in the gap between his teeth.

For decades, you carry this story because there's an animal in her you

understand. It is neither good nor bad

                                        what happens to that girl.

There's a young man, a teenager, standing next to me on the train. The arms of his sweater are too short and pilling. His hood is pulled over his eyes and, as the train shakes on, he presses his body—face-first—against the sliding door. Muttering.

I'm sure he's looking at me. I'm uneasy, the grey fabric bumps along his sweater and thin skin around his knuckles iridescent, reminiscent of a thumb sliding out of a child's mouth. I'm not sure he's looking at me. He's unwell. He must be unwell, different.

Penis. Take my dick. Fat Bitch. Take my. Take my dick. Take it. Penis. Fat Bitch. Take my

Even after he leaves, even when the train car is empty

Take my dick. Fat Bitch. Take my dick. Ta ta take it.

Found

.

F Train last week . . . - w4w
Reply to: pers-375453454@craigslist.org
Date: 2007-07-16, 8:12 PM EDT

Me: Black woman
You: Asian woman

You showed me your beautiful vagina and we touched. I fingered you
for six stops. You came, kissed me on the cheek and exited the train.

My heart has never beaten faster.

Where are you?

Vasilyssa Wants to Know What Love Is

Who loved whom
more when undeniable

who tilled whom
widened her effusion

webbed hand, shadowscape
of mother birch & broken horses.

Field of women unfurled,
young fern

I wanted
to know what my body knew

what spiders made a night pool
of my mouth

while I slept wet
without closure.

This marshland
mosquito lullaby

each time I pitched my sorrow tent
you sent me thunder. So thunder,

what is fact? A flat black rock
I lie under.

L. visits me for nine days. She comes bearing
six airplane-safe bottles of prickly pear juice

she harvested herself, small round
pears, and coffee beans meant for her mother.

She asks why I have so much rope around my bed and
when her clothes are fresh from the wash, she
strips my rope and uses it for clothing line.

Over drinks at a bar called *Bar,* I read her
Bishop's "At the Fishhouses." I'm unsure
what compels me or why she's crying.

Something about *principal beauty,* the glittering dead fish, the sea lion surfacing

again and again. I remember the Tender Prince,
how we sat at the same bar, read the same poem,

wept. Night, I fuck L.'s face and she begins to hum.

Nor'easter and new moon, my mother's birthday,
we ride home, road made of snow.

                Mama's sister Anya (may the ground be kind to her)

                  would waggle her purse up at the crescent light,

             barely waxing, and cry *богиня! Ты меня слышишь?*

—according to my mother,
who fishes cash from her pocket

        mimics her dead sister—

             Goddess! Do you hear me? Goddess! Give me money.

Everyone is laughing
rummaging for quarters.

Twenty, sunburnt at Brooklyn Pride.   Park Slope dense with rainbow flags,

a woman's hand

                                        pulls me. In her tent, my palm says it all:

Your love line, cursed. The diagnosis: *black bile. They'll all leave you.*

The cure? *$10.99 plus $5 for the reading.*

When I was loved I lived at the edge of rooftops

                                                grew my hair long.

When the boat came

                        a lantern, a foghorn,

a death, my swan in her mouth.   I took the boat. I let the boat take me.

I'm on the sixth floor, Jenny's on third. Fourth: a woman wearing a muumuu, fat Chihuahua in her arms; Fifth: a white-haired man with eyes we never see and his home-care worker, their dog black with teeth.

Night, Jenny and I squat in the staircases between. She wears a T-shirt covered in cats and rhinestone hearts. It clings to her breasts, which are changing. She smokes a cigarette or we talk about boys or we are fourteen years old, sulky with virginity.

Tomorrow, we'll go to the beach. At the beach, the same man will appear again. He'll park his towel behind ours. His dick will sun beside him, a fat lizard. The lifeguard will tell us to move.

Salty in the elevator, we'll recount the injustice. On the handrail, a pair of panties will swing innocuous, a different color than the week before and without owner.

Coney Island Vasya

Call the dark bird home the way you call a little girl
back from the water

Sheepshead Bay, summer, and seagulls caw
                                        circling her squawk

She gives herself to the sea   She is the salt house
                        of herself
Ocean above   Ocean below

Wave and wave again, a gull breaks water
                                feeds on what she finds

Your first child will be born with the head of a fish; too
much water bore you up, well, it would be hard on a
child dressed in seaweed, black stones, scales.

Everything lies down the same:
                        sunlight and the angle it makes

Her bathing suit, coral red
                                she walks the beach

One seashell stacks into the other, two men follow her
along the bank until their shadows drown

How does the seagull sense the crab below sea foam
and silt? One deal is enough

She knows their call and that is all she knows

I've been to Riis Beach twice. First time? Preteen, flat as the surface of a lake. But the ocean! Wild there—unkind too. Aunt Anya was with us. Wide bank of cellulite, her behind. Her face? All nose and grimace. Twenty years my mother's senior, terrifying. Once, Anya dragged me apartment to apartment, each full of Babas playing lotto, betting nickels. Riis Beach? Right, that. A large wave came, undressed me. I was pulling my top on

—there's nothing there, for fuck's sake—Anya laughed, slapped me in my nothing.

A decade later I returned. Someone called it a gay beach. I saw some dicks hanging, dykes marinating jerk chicken. I took a walk by myself and found a seashell, blue lightning whelk, large as my hand.

*As **if it were against better judgment.** Cold, dark, deep, and absolutely clear, the clear grey icy water . . .* She was both woman and quartz, a universe refracted with pain and methadone. Once, with purpose, I pressed my palm against her spine, the moon gathered in me. I watched her back swallow my hand, wrist-deep, a ghost hand. She was born in the year of the water dog so I called her *Water Dog.* When her tongue lapped my cunt, an abandoned kit burrowed wool blankets and slept in me.

When she penetrated me, hard, like I asked her to, I shuddered and shut down, crying. *Flowing and flown.*

My twenty-fifth birthday, one month after my father died, one month after my girlfriend left, she came to me. Tight, her hand around my throat.

Found

Bek
January 7, 2015, 02:48:35 AM
mobile 1(917) xxx-xxxx

(voice mail)

[. . .] *just take half a Xanax and write a list of little dreams. Like butter-fly. What is that?*
Bearhead.

I want to know a lot of animals before I die.

After *Manuela*, a telenovela dubbed in Russian, CTC broadcasts a documentary.

One pasty man in his forties cites 1990s raves as the beginning of gay culture.

Truly, he claims, *everyone was so colorful, like aliens landing.*

It's the first time I see gay people on RT without blood on their faces.

My mother is beside me in her bed, a couch unfolded.

TV screen the only light.

I can't see her face.

She can't see mine.

Tomorrow's a good day to visit your father's grave, she lets me know
                                              she's awake and watching.

Vasilyssa Considers the Dark Path

Everyone knows you can't

                         enter a house with no doors

Slow rot between her throat

                         and heart, it's not darkness

that scares her. Bones glint

                         moonlight and bonesorrow

The house is always spinning,

                         the house wants a song, sing

and it opens the house is not

                         a woman is not not a woman

(It was easy, you know. We sat across from each other for a long time not watching the TV. She said *come closer* and I said *no* you *come closer*. In touching we opened a door we could not close and did not want to. I said *sleep in my bed* but I meant tonight not every night; still there she was every night. I just kept sinking to the bottom like a stone. I just lay there wet and without thoughts.)

In the beginning, a girl was

                         very wise and very beautiful

Good with her hands, she

                         slept, soft-cheeked on a horse's

pulse. She knew nothing

                         about animals, only gentleness

a cat's tongue in the milk

                         lapping. She loved that way too

(I kept calling you. I kept calling you even though I forgot how telephones work how time how to make sound I kept calling you I would say *I'm nothing I'm a stone I'm covered in bad milk I saw my father's blue waterlogged body and I couldn't touch now untouchable forever* and you would say *O it's hot here I'll come soon I have to go now I can't talk*

too long I have to conduct this very important interview with
these people they're so old and they could die I would come
but why is that girl in your bed why is she there?)

What built the house also dug
                              the grave. She sings the song
and loves death's hands, how
                    they mind their own business

He begins by sliding the edge against stone until it sparks. That's my father paring the apple. His long fingers catch the skin like a prize. My father tilting the blade, sharp against each pencil, bringing the color back. When he's through, he rests the knife on the kitchen windowsill, gated and diamond-crossed, stained from cigarettes, boardwalk air. Evening, he places an apple, quartered, beside the pencils and looks at me with gladness because I've asked for such small things.

I ask my mother for something small I can hold on to. She sends me his wallet and a stopped pocket watch. *That's all,* she said.

The wallet? Leather Americana embossed with flowers, a name that's not his. Painful empty. Months later, I find one two-dollar bill in a secret pocket.

He kept it that way.

Even dead, he's got me laughing, a wallet named Peter and an antique bill. I cut my hair and it feels like crying.

What I want is a kitchen with good sunlight, a kerchief for my table, and my father's samovar, gold with blue flowers.

What I have is his white ceramic cup painted a Soviet winter scene, permanently stained, and black lace from the week we buried him.

I forget how to make dinner. The wrong girl puts her hand inside me. Damn it. What I want is good light and something clean.

My brother bought her from a drunk at the market, brought her home crammed in a cardboard box punched with holes. Pretend it was my birthday, I was the four-year-old she was meant for. Fistful of feathers: my cockatiel, my familiar.

Bright scarf, she unspooled, yellow-green and creased, her wings warped. Teaching her to fly, I made a branch of my chubby arms, nest of my hair. Papa took her up in his large hands and whispered (we thought her a boy), *Кеша хороший, Кеша хороший.*

How she learned to be good: say you are good. How did a bird love me? Midflight. In the crook of my arm, neck, cooing and curled in. How did a bird leave me? I boarded a plane. I gave her away.

All night the squirrels scratch their way in
                  attic window, bushy tails flicking,
                  rubber mallet marks the ceiling, my warning

unheeded. I came here alone, years ago. Past lumberyard—wet
smell of cedar and fir.

Cockatiel cage nailed outside some apartment door, red-bloom
trumpet vines cascading the entryway

—now gone. November—you came
with your books, your bitch, your kitchen goods, and I made room.

                        It's been months now. Don't come home.

Kitchen

You want the crying girl the   one who kept walking
        into water, salt pool larger and larger
                                    around her neck.
Daisy crown in her fist, clump of sad weeds.

Vasilyssa the wise throws a comb behind her,
                wakes a birch forest, keeps running.

Vasilyssa floats   into your dreams, waterlogged,
and pockets your hair in fistfuls.
            You're a doll in her hand, hair and straw, slag.

Every childhood has a kitchen, a floor for dog scraps,
                            an oven you can't touch.

Vasilyssa the brave enters Baba's house and sits down
at her table.   Here she is

hysteric, woman   cracking eggshells underwater
until all the pieces float.   She's lifting

the egg up to your mouth   wet, slippery, born.

You'll be my cumhole, won't you?

She's not asking, her pussy   slicking

Her mouth rich, butter,

tongue fills up my, dumbs

belt lick, pliant lightning   (say *thank you*)

(say *please*)

Before dinner, only hours ago,

told me not to

look at her that way

I slipped off   my want, sweater

in a room, sweltering.

Our meal came, one dish   salmon skin

I split

with a dull knife

Said   *I prefer ma'am*   (an instruction)   to some butch across the table

who lapped it up

Copernicus Deli. I slice German ham so precisely
                    I could kiss the woman who
                    bears witness.

We gasp together. *Nothing could be more perfect,* she claims.

At 5 a.m., I was having beautiful sex, my ex writes back
when I text her my morning dream

                    in which she is a body
                    of yellow light pouring
                    into me. I ring

my customer up, I wipe meat juice from my blade.

Valentine's family arrived in America a year after mine. After school he comes and we do homework in the kitchen; I don't have a desk. Papa makes dinner, kotletki, and our hands get greasy with meat.

The bedroom I share with my parents: mahogany veneer queen, dresser, and vanity. My bed's in the corner, a grey foldout chair covered in lightning bolts. We rub Barbies, we play teacher and pupil, we play whatever I want. Valentine annoys me.

Valentine scribbles *I will not bother girls* fifty times with my no. 2 pencil because I said so. He has to practice his English. My purple turtleneck fits him fine so he wears it home. I like seeing him in it. I like knowing it's mine.

Valentine's number feels good in the rotary, purrs after every turn. The cord curls around my finger, that's nice too. All the girls at school say *you have such nice boyfriend.*

I tell them: *He can be your boyfriend also, ask.*

In the *New Yorker,* **a poem** about original sin or picnic baskets.
　　　　I'm at the same café drinking the same drink I'm always drinking.

They've got cowhide scraps on the metal chairs. It's luxurious.
　　　　You're texting about cumming in my mouth, and outside

a woman cradles flowers in her arms. Stepping out of the deli next door,
a girl takes a long drag of her cigarette, twice. She snuffs smoke with her

heel, returns to work. Suddenly all shoes fit me. I consider how many men
I'd let cum on me if you were watching. I'm the only woman you're with

who doesn't take dick and you dream of defiling me. Just last week you
finger-fucked me while pushing 70 MPH on the freeway.

We discuss (if ever) an accident:
　　　　　　　　　　　　　What if I'm unable to move? I ask.
　　　　　　　　　　　　　　　　　Perfect, you say.
　　　　　　　　　　　　　Besides the fucking? I persist.
　　　　　　　　　　　　　　The fucking is the thing.

I try to recall at what precise moment **the voices of women who sound like birds** began to appeal to me.   Parted beak. Throat an open tunnel. Once, I was

a server. A girl waved me over and asked me how one eats whitefish on the bone.

Part the meat gently so that the bones rise. Mind loose ones still clinging to the flesh. Trust your mouth.

                                                            You're so glad I'm here

in bed, my small birds in your hands.   *You said the fucking was the thing,*
                                               I say, I thought the fucking was the thing.

              O, you sigh. *O, that breaks my heart.*

The Key to All Locks Is a Fearless Heart

Everything wants back to Brighton Beach.　　Three girls enter the Q train
littered with dried herring.　　　*The needle you seek is inside a golden egg,*
　　　　　a mallard, a hare, a crystal chest, the tip of a pine—respectively.

Three girls enter the Q train to Coney Island.　　They cannot sit. Herring
is everywhere; they pick it up, take photographs.　　A man wants the girls
to take him, grips herring with his teeth.

Go there　　　　*I know not where*　　　*Bring me back a thing I lack.*

Vasilyssa rides the back of a black bear forward, knows hunger and cold.
Vasilyssa rides the back of a black bear to the right, her horse drops dead.
Vasilyssa rides the back of a black bear left and dies so the horse may live.

What is the fastest thing on earth? Dear, life is not the only thing on earth.

In the thrice-nine land, at the edge of the world where the sorrel horse rises

　　　　　Vasya, brush bats from Baba's hair. Her cat will scratch you,
　　　her dog will bite you, her birch will lash you and put out your eyes.

Vasilyssa knows night gallops　　　　　　　a Friesian cannot harm her.
Three girls enter the Q train
　　　　　wearing wedding gowns from the bottom of the river.

Remember each horse that came to you　　　what did you do for them?

Weekends with my mother were old wet rags slung over a broom, brush broken off. After days slicing meat thin as paper, enduring baba after baba, lacquered fingertips against her deli case: *Devushka! Give me fresh cuts!* After evenings on her knees for Hasidic housewives, toothbrush-scrubbing tile floors, she rose Saturdays ready to keep house. School days, I was my father's daughter but Saturdays

she tempered my hands into women's hands. What a good хозяйка knew how to do: *pull the broom toward yourself,* she said, grabbing it from me, sweat slicking insides of her arms. Acrid. *Each stroke and sweep should be firm, have purpose.*

But, like, where is the body?

>> Girl in Feminist Literary Theory wants to know. She's got

precise long ringlets, tendency toward baby-doll shirts. *Yes, and opacity?*

PhDs round the table join in, *What is the opacity of the body?*
>> *And the writer . . . is she here in the text?*
> (Hermeneutics) *Where is the body? Where is the body?*

All poets on standby: we prod our bran muffins,
plop baby carrots back into Tupperware,   our underarms cold with irritation.

The professor trails white chalk across her grey skirt, filling up the blackboard
with heteroromance. Oh?
>> Tell me more about that marriage plot,
>> I am licking my fingers and picking up crumbs.

I'm crying fruit tears inside the Goblin Market. I am Lizzie calling Laura up the
garden. *Did you miss me? Come and kiss me. Never mind my bruises, hug me, kiss
me, suck my juices.*

Squeez'd from goblin fruits for you, goblin pulp and goblin dew.

Pablo slides his finger through a hole in my tights. He won't fuck me because *I'm not that kind of girl.* He plays electric guitar; I jerk him off right in his pants. His forehead gets damp and I smear my mouth on it like his mother.

Pablo drops out sophomore year, gets arrested for trying to mug a woman. I'm not his girlfriend but I make hummus with his mother. I feel lonely for her. Tonight, Pablo calls because he loves me. He tells me he's god, tells me all about B—

how *she wore a skirt so short her pussy hung out,* how he fucked her *just to show her what a slut she is.*

First week of high school, the Towers fall. We're in the auditorium, waiting. Simon sits in my lap and pricks my finger. He puts the bloody mess in his mouth. I don't know him. I could sleep for one hundred years; I'm faint, that's how come he's my boyfriend.

A date we go on: Natural History Museum; he fingers me right below dead-eyed elephants. I take myself home, head hot against subway glass.

At lunch, my friend pulls me aside. *Simon says you're dumb as shit but at least you're pretty.* I pass Simon a note: it's over. Simon garbage cans my friend, fractures her arm.

Simon dates this girl I know. One night, at L'amours, a metal show, his girl minds the heat. I lend her my tank top. She never gives it back; she tells me she likes to wear it when he fucks her.

Vasya, in Bed

If you fall asleep now, all the mice will find your bed.
Drawn to the warm life in you, they'll spend the night

power grooming your small patches of fur   nibbling
on your overgrown toenails.   You don't want that.

It's too close.   Stay awake, Vasya.
No one's coming.   Breeze is cold.
Pull the covers over your ears.   Not a woman.
                    Just the shape of a woman.

Weight presses down on your duvet-lump body   push
the word *go* from your ghost-wrapped throat. She'll go.

Not all ghosts mean trouble   —you could let her stay.
                (To aid sleep, recite the Cyrillic alphabet.)

At the foot of your bed   something.
Close your window, keep water by.

That's a frog's croak.   That's your body.
                That's a night bird.

Floppy disks, squares of delicate plastic, hidden in the cubby of my desk. I run each one. Here, amateur photo of a woman, feathered hair, tank top hiked up, breasts like too-ripe cantaloupes. This one, I can't look—

Printing cantaloupe woman takes a long time. The pinpoint ink dots are an '80s Kodak schematic. *Dear Eric,* I use my favorite jelly pen, *our eyes met while you were standing in the snack bar line. That's a nice white turtleneck. Also, I saw you by Sizzling Bikes riding a go-cart. I live upstairs. Do you live far? I want to come over. You can travel the valley of my breasts*—I write in the valley of cantaloupe breasts, *valley* because I've read lots of Danielle Steel since they're right by the YA section.

The note, folded a tight wand, tucks perfectly into my fairy-tale collection (where it will vibrate for the next decade, a vestige of twelve-year-old lust). I'm brave but I'm not stupid; I find Eric online. I know how this goes, do it with strangers all the time.

My secret screen name: Sweetgirl87. What Eric writes: *A/S/L, shaved or unshaved?*

Eric lives above a small clinic on Ocean Parkway. Eric says *meet me by the yellow deli.* We walk together, Eric: 5'5", skin the color of milky coffee and green glass eyes. I'm too tall, pale, padded strapless bra, baby-pink tank top. I float around his room, touch his things (a gun . . . is that really a gun?). I trace them gently like a girl.

Come into the bathroom (it's dark) *sit on my lap* (I sit) *tell me what you want.* Eric's friends come over, high school boys, brown and long-limbed. They're easy, fill the room. One cocks his head: *This your girl? Nah,* Eric answers, rolling blunts, not looking up.

You don't love me, you say, and deflate
our air mattress, meeting me at the fold.

              We're in a bad lesbian performance piece.

You don't eat the sandwich I make you.
I puncture your yoga ball. Or, the dog did.

              This is a drawing of the dog.
          I meant to watch something and be still
                 for a long time.

I'm not sure what belongs to me.

        It's your money
            stop asking me what you mean.

Porcelain skunk, perfect Q-tip holder.
Ceramic parrot, good for something.

      If you don't trust me with this cup then wrap it yourself.

The dog hasn't stopped barking in hours—anxious.

       I know you can lift the chair, what you can do
            is not the point.

I've really been working on my orgasmic meditation, my ex confides.
*If the instructor touches my clit in a way that agitates me, I just pretend
I like it, and then I do.*

She sends me a link to a TED talk on orgasmic meditation.
We talk for a bit about her recent breakup.
It's the same TED talk link she sent me two months ago.

Thank God for Jen, she whispers, and she means her best friend.
I brought a woman home last night just to talk, she tells me.
She reminded me of you.

If a Suitor Should Come

The morning? Not good (but wise). Vasilyssa
doesn't get a flying ship, a charming chimney
sweep, or patty-cake games on the windowsill
with her hair unbraided.

Daylight Vasilyssa's a frog; she lives in a marsh,
she can't fling her china from a shuttered tower
like an exclamation point.

In the garden: three cages.

One Copper One Silver One Gold.
Copper Crow Silver Jackdaw Gold Firebird.
Vasya drinks the water of life from Firebird's beak.
Bring back the bird but leave the cord that binds it.

The evening? Unwise. Vasilyssa washes her hair
in water boiled with corn husks. Weaves carpets
of night flowers, throws a moon from her crown.
Vasilyssa sees her betrothed. There he is.

In a mirror, a flame, a bouillon cup, but
never at her eye level.
A test of honor, Vasya
throws her beloved in boiling water.

Night ritual: She drapes cheesecloth on her face,
bugs settle there.   Not hungry, she closes
her eyes; buzzing is an ocean over her.

Red kerchief, wrap
the firebird.
Stars hang like oranges,
her skin a milky river   the marsh makes green.

If Vasilyssa Is the Suitor

The cock crows.   Vasilyssa cuts her hair.
Triangles dangle from the tips of her braids and
                  she cries into them, a kerchief.

No dress or dressage   Vasilyssa makes off
on a horse, in tunic.   Vasilyssa has 99 problems
      but needs one more to make an even number.

If there is a kingdom then Vasilyssa comes.

      Ride straight ahead, know hunger and cold.
      Ride to the right, live but your steed will die.
      Ride left and die, though your steed shall live.

If there's no kingdom   the woods will do.
          If Vasilyssa wears a witch's cloak
to the witch's clearing   they are both crones.
If the hut dances on two fowl legs, Vasilyssa calls
from her deep, dark throat:
           Turn your door toward me little hut
           little hut. Turn your face toward me
           and away from the forest.

If she enters the hut, she'll pet three cats, each time
ask for a woman.
          She'll expect a witch:
dead hair, breasts to her waist, a chin that curls up,
and nose that curls down.   Who comes?

A crescent-faced Baba, hair woven with blue roses,
        Oh Vasilyssa, the joke will be on her.

I'm the grey skirt that trails behind me, ripping open. Sophomore year, college, coral ring left in my mailbox from a woman I've never fucked and am trying to forget. Days open and close bone-cold. My mentor left me her book at her deathbed: *A Family of Strangers*. I ruin it sloppy crying.

Beatrice, Dusty writes, *you're mine,* like she's Dante. It's Myspace; she says whatever she wants. Once I watched her prance a field, topless, in goat pants: Pan. Now we haunt the internet. It works like this: we know each other's moans before we know each other's mouths. We build a citadel out of expectation. She sends me her shirt rank with sweat and amber oil. I keep it under my pillow, huff it in my sleep. Webcam on, I brace my leg on the desk.

Three-hour plane ride from New York to Austin, bouquet of long-stemmed lollipops bright stained glass in my lap. She's wearing a tight '70s white linen pantsuit. Her hair's tinged with blue. We kiss and it's clumsy, sweet. Her small black truck bumps and speeds against the Texas afternoon. We corral our breaths and feign shyness; broncs in a bucking chute.

A girl brings me home to nothing. I thought it was her last name but
it's her occupation. Peruke: archaic for wig. We're living in olden times

where every bar takes only cash, every window displays a bad invention.
Once she worked in the Natural History Museum in a den of dead butterflies.

Now, wigs everywhere, head full of colors lying flat. There are drugs
that call your body, graceful leaf, slowly to the ground. *Now you're talking*

my language, sipping beer and holding up opposite walls. I ask her why
she's not kissing me. All the butterflies in the room are choking on pot smoke.

I'm penetrating her and we both have our clothes on. She wants to see my body
and it's over before it started. That's the thing about any room

where the way in is also the way out. We midnight deli on the corner
with no street signs, busted lights, get our bagels toasted with cream cheese

and salmon. It tastes like salty cardboard. I let her pay because I bought the beer
and, anyway, I like to be thanked in one way or another. Like girls are taught to.

2:00 on a Thursday, everyone stuffing their
mouths with twenty-dollar sandwiches.

> I've run up those stairs over a dozen times
> in the past ten minutes, my knees know it.

Left behind: a table peppered with pieces
of meat, sopping napkins, one chair
covered in crayon scrawl. No tip.

> In my blue gloves, waste loses meaning.
> Shape to like shape, stack. My body, broom,
> slinks in and out, gathers garbage.

At the dishwashing station, I slip cups into
cup holes. Shawna, short-order butch whispers,

> *Damn girl, smile,* as she brushes by me.
> Spit and soda mix, drip down my arms.

Somebody is singing Lesley Gore's "You Don't Own Me,"
badly, sort of shrill and declarative.

I'm working on nothing

waiting for my lover

who is not always kind to me but,

and this is Lesley Gore's ghost coming on,

I'm young and I want to be loved.

When you are sleeping with someone
more accomplished, your name is *Yes.*

I'm the beaded curtain jangling and parted on the reading stage.

Why is it here? What is the purpose of

beads? *Oh, and this is . . . um. Yes.* Tacky.

So long my neck coils tight, won't loose.
So long she varies what she places on my
ass: paperwork, books, belt unfastened.

> It's not awful, aching arc of my spine, neck,
> floor wronging my knees. Weak. On all fours

I suck her clit—*gentle*—she slaps me.
I imagine whipped tips of soft-serve.

> Stay in my place.

She three-fingers me, keeps me open, crawls me over like an owner.

She loves me I know

> as if love is matter and I hold it.
> Shallow, bowl of my back.

Vasya/Venus/Violet/Violent

Winged come land   out, away from sex
roost my mouth   leaving it

black bat cloud   flower of it
fat rubber shaft

four-letter word   a profusion of flowers
four-finger gag

come cave cunt-shaped   it was these lips she rouged
lipstain-smeared rag   as if a mouth

Strike stone, wood bone,   mobile flesh
come flame the pit   flesh made of elastic

turn chicken spit   to heighten her value:
and split each lip   resistance

Come switch   flowers which shone
Come switch   in the dark for a woman
Comes/witch   who shone in the dark

and watch: the mirror bends, O, bed-shaped boat   the ass, turned
Knot, Sailor, tight around the throat   loses shape, drawn apart

Here, brass foot   convulsive gesture: pulling
anchor, ankle swell   pulling the branch, the boy

Come brute come violent   whose skin, tender
violet, knuckle-rough   as a woman's

I'm infant blond: weak at the crown,   precarious

Received

RE: *Dyke Needs Man to Fuck Her Girlfriend-* W4M   6:28 PM *(4 hours ago)*

FROM: *Robert Mc*****<b9813a9c8b0aff3d7ab@reply.craigslist.org >*

My name is Rob I just got out of jail I'm hot out of the box I'll fuck and suck like an animal there's no stopping me I'm going crazy for sex.

Adaptation is a kind of trauma, I tell my boss when he mentions my lack of
   accent.

Some of us have no traceable affect, have learned our language from strangers.

He nods, shows my friend how to use the meat slicer, the scale.

This kind of work will be good for you, he explains.

In Poland, we were young engineers,
                    we worked with the soldiers and dug trenches in the woods.

By water, teenagers smoke weed and loosies in the brambles.
Women come home to houses by the tracks.

Come back, you said.   Facing backward,

Long Island railroading to you, three chickens peck around
an SUV parked in the yard.   This great American landscape,

I'm drinking bottled water I bought over at McDonald's

at Atlantic Mall.   I got a small Coke, too
but the boy only charged me for one item.   Do you think

it's my beauty that compelled him or

that I was so thirsty. I don't know why I got a Coke anyway. Never mind.
I love this part, the sun sets yolk-orange

on the Atlantic, O lover, clouds dramatic and without shape.

Last week I packed my life and you lifted me out from one town
to another.   Baltimore burned with grief.

We cleaned the windowpanes   and drank Miller High Life.

The mattress we spent months fucking on, strapped to your car,
vibrated so hard on the highway we couldn't bear it.   But once

you tie a mattress to your car and go, you're tied to the mattress.
You can't toss it. Illegal.   The whole world is on fire

and it's not new. Another rapist won the Pulitzer. The abducted
Somali girls returned pregnant, almost all.

French peacekeepers took advantage of the boy refugees. NPR
does a feature on a feel-good radio host.

Ineffectual, too much lift.   We bought more ratchet straps,
we tightened the rope.   We're poets, thought physics

an education in mythology.   For hours, we held the mattress
to the roof rack with our hands   knowing it did nothing.

X

A twin heart,
a pill and put
your things. I
to be
cock alive
large and
in color. You
over
I put on X-
Spex, Poly
a teenage
a soft light
brighter. I'm
with her
gaze and big
I'm stroking
arm so soft,
you're
Everything,
vinyl
the drag of
feet back and
The sadness

I take
on all
want
close! Your
from me,
incongruous
fall
delighting.
Ray
Styrene,
comet,
getting
in love
avoidant
braces.
your
long,
beholding.
her
dress,
her
forth.

a purse
spare change in,
small mushrooms
on my father's
grave. My mother's
eye milking over.
The dick and harness,
you like it and that
makes me like it.
All of a sudden
nothing
is not beautiful. You're
very close to me
like this. Hold my jaw,

I keep

each song is a lizard
on the branch
changing
shape. She loves me
because my heart is
good under your heart.
Open the window,
close the window,
wonderful window
where all the air comes through.

Drunk, one sneaker over the other, мишка косолапый,
something stuck to his lower lip, he loads my bag into the trunk.

In the car, clean turns   (ex-cabbie can do this in his sleep).

Volume turned up   *Hate it or love it, the underdog's*
                                    on top—Dima only knows the chorus.

He makes guttural noises for the rest.   He smokes one cigarette.
We're on the Belt, wind whips back the ash.

                                        Where we are going? He forgot.

Poem about a deposit box with _____ inside.
(*are you scared?*   *i'm not scared.*   *you look scared.*)

We're on the Belt, Nassau/Van Wyck.
                              We can get a quick bite, if you want.
Another cigarette.   *Write a script, call it "You're Good*
                                        and I'm Bad."

Tears pocket where his glasses meet his face,
                    my hand on his hand—it's awkward.

                              Do you know about me?

He means: Disavowal, a brother whose ax wants for wood
                              and returns without, worse.

Bad techno, old coffee in the cup holder,   big blue glass eye
                                        for protection.

              лапша на уши: Good people do bad things, I say.
                    He doesn't nod or look at me.

Poem about my father going into the ground:
                    dirt on his hands, my brother turns to me and asks
                              Don't you need forgiveness?

I was a warm live thing that wanted

> to be loved above all others. Seer. With my father's
> playing cards spread semi-circle around me. A hand

hovering over each for an answer.

> O. Hot hand. Current buzzing in my palm. Currant,
> blue and bitter in my mouth. Some song

from childhood. Song wearing beaded bonnet.

> Kalinka! Kalinka! So close to my own name—forget
> it. Someone I love

Someone I love, burst berry in the mouth,

> hand on fire, open circuit. Circle broken. It's all up
> and given.

Photo of the moon. It's barely a moon,

> some hole ripped out of black paper.

Notes

"There are things I will not share with everyone." —Adrienne Rich

Return

"The wave always returns, and always returns a different wave" is a line I've excerpted from Marina Tsvetaeva's lyric essay "Poets with History and Poets without History," collected in *Art in the Light of Conscience: Eight Essays on Poetry* and translated by Angela Livingstone (2010). The essay collection is a testament to not only Tsvetaeva's mythomania (which is palpable) but also the means by which—in a time of great spiritual and material scarcity—she constructed a phenomenology of ethno-embodiment that was at once rooted and yielding.

Received

This poem is a found poem and an entry into my erotic archive. This poem is an email from my first girlfriend wherein a suicidal narrator (Edna) is used as a stand-in for the speaker (my gf) who is not in love with me so much as she is in love with drowning. This email was written shortly after we fucked for the first time while Tegan and Sara's "My Number" played in the background—which is a tangent you will understand if you were also a lesbian in 2004. This email poem is a classic example of projection. This email contains excerpts from Rosemary Franklin's article on Kate Chopin's *The Awakening*, excerpts the speaker never attributed to their source.

Tenderness

This book, a YA novel by Robert Cormier, boasts this lovely description on Amazon:

> EIGHTEEN-YEAR-OLD ERIC HAS just been released from juvenile detention for murdering his mother and stepfather. Now he's looking for some tenderness—tenderness he finds in caressing and killing beautiful girls. Fifteen-year-old Lori has run away from home again. Emotionally naive but sexually precocious, she is also looking for tenderness—tenderness she finds in Eric. Will Lori and Eric be each other's salvation or destruction?

Found

Another entry into my erotic archive, a collection of events mostly but not exclusively sexual in nature, which shaped my sense of self as sexed. This ad is one of many Craigslist w4w missed-connection ads (a moment of silence, please, for all good things that are gone) I collected as a baby dyke, hoping to one day find someone hoping to find me—an evidence of beholding. This entry is particularly striking due to the women's shamelessness, which is a kind of miracle, and the writer's attention to detail (six stops!). I lived off the F train; I wondered after them.

L. visits me for nine days

Variations of this poem have appeared as "Dear Would-Be Wife" in my chapbook, *One Above One Below: Positions & Lamentations* (YesYes Books 2018), and online. Variations of the experiences rendered in this poem have been wrought out with/onto several women and GNC people who, no doubt, are no longer interested in hearing me read Bishop's "At the Fishhouses" aloud to them. That is a shame but not a great shame.

Found

This entry into the erotic archive, a voice mail from one of my oldest friends, is an emotional entry. This voice mail is one of many small tendernesses we have learned to give each other in a world that so often proves sugarless, in a world where my friends were (as Audre Lorde once wrote) never meant to survive. I love you, Bek. I all the animals you.

But, like, where is the body?

The mining of opacity, as regarded in this poem, stems from reading the work of Daphne Brooks, specifically her essay "'The Deeds Done in My Body': Black Feminist Theory, Performance, and the Truth about Adah Isaacs Menken." In her essay, Brooks argues that "the opaque operates as a method of contestation and invention for the public, performative, and racially ambiguous nineteenth-century female figure." In my feminist literary theory class, full of (mostly white and racially ambiguous) twenty-first-century female figures, it appeared that the primary concern was finding Brooks's body in the text—a sad but not altogether unexpected state of intellectual affairs—and simply repeating the word *opacity* over and over as if to masticate and consume Brooks's meaning.

Thinking about the body, where it is and where it is not, I was reminded of another late nineteenth-century female figure, Christina Rossetti, whose poem "Goblin Market" (first published in 1861) is excerpted here. This poem serves to offer the queer erotic body (of Rossetti and of her "characters") to the reader; it is an example of queer opacity. It is also an example of MFA candidates' interior state when surrounded by PhDs.

I've really been working on my orgasmic meditation
Should you want to watch the TED talk, it's titled "Orgasm: The Cure for Hunger in the Western Woman," given by Nicole Daedone in 2011, and it's on TEDxSF.

Somebody is singing
Lesley Gore was a young lesbian who loved to be young.

Vasya/Venus/Violet/Violent
This poem is a sweeping and somewhat irreverent erasure of Anaïs Nin's *Delta of Venus* (1977), which, for your information, did not rock my world. What did rock my world is the song "Violet" by Hole (1994), in which Courtney sings "want to give the violent more violets" but which I have always heard as "want to give a violet more violent." This poem is a violet more violent. How rarely are the letters *v*, *i*, and *o* placed together, how beautifully they wind up in the mouth.

Received
This, too, lights up my erotic archive. I submit it as an evidence and, clearly, a missed opportunity.

Drunk, one sneaker over the other
| мишка косолапый: | Clumsy bear (this is an image of inelegance encoded into Russian children) |
| лапша на уши: | Noodle on the ears (An idiomatic phrase it is said like this, "Oh come on! Don't hang noodles on my ears!" The speaker, in this case, is not interested in your bullshit. In my case, I am the one hanging the noodles.) |

Acknowledgments

Versions of these poems have previously appeared in the following publications:

One Above One Below: Positions & Lamentations | YesYes Books | 3/6/2018

"X" | Poetry Project | 2/12/2018

"Return" | Academy of American Poets, poets.org | 2/9/2018

"There's always a forest I know" | Nomadic Ground Poetry | 8/1/2017

"By water" published as "American Landscape" | *Day One* | 4/24/2017

"Tenderness," "My brother" & "Vasya/Venus/Violet/Violent" | *PEN America* | 9/22/2016

"I was a warm live thing" | *The Adroit Journal* | 8/11/2016

"On the Brighton Beach boardwalk" | *Boston Review* | 5/09/2016

"Vasilyssa Considers the Dark Path" | *The James Franco Review* | 4/10/2016

"As if it were against better judgment," "Adaptation is a kind of trauma" & *"So long my neck coils tight"* | *Bedfellows* | 4/04/2016

"I'm the grey skirt that trails behind me, ripping open" & "Somebody is singing" | *GlitterMOB* | 1/06/2016

"Valentine" | *Pouch* | 7/15/2015

"Kitchen" | *Winter Tangerine* | 4/15/2015

"L. visits me for nine days," "All night the squirrels" & *"You don't love me,* you say, and deflate" | *Newfound* | Spring 2015

"Eric lives above a small clinic" & "First week of high school, the Towers fall" | *CutBack* | 8/20/2014

"He begins by sliding the edge against stone" & "I ask my mother for something small" | *Muzzle* | 6/13/2014

"Body, mud-wet field," "We go around in a circle," "High school wasn't always two towers crashing" & "I've been to Riis Beach" | *NAILED* | 6/02/2014

"I've really been working on my orgasmic meditation" published as "Girl-talk" | *The Feminist Wire* | 12/11/2013

"Twenty, sunburnt at Brooklyn Pride" & "I saw a woman lunge into the pit" published as "Summons" | *PANK* | October 2013

For publishing my first chapbook, *One Above One Below: Positions &* *Lamentations,* where some of these poems appear, I praise Katherine (KMA) Sullivan for her unwavering support and commitment to a world where poetry is supreme.

For believing in this book and helping it come to life, I owe a great deal to the Coffee House Press team but especially to my editor, Erika Stevens, whose attentive and tireless devotion to the work is nothing short of heroic.

Of course, my endless appreciation goes to the Helen Zell Writers' Program (University of Michigan MFA). I am enthusiastically indebted to Laura Kasischke, for her keen mystic eye, and Ray McDaniel, who might be the saving grace for Scorpio men everywhere. Without you, this book would not be. Thanks to my cohort, but especially to my beloved Claire Skinner, Airea Dee Matthews, Bruce Lack, Camille Beckman, Tina Richardson, Mary-Alice Daniel, Megan Levad, francine j. harris, Audra Puchalski, Aeryne James Hixon, Ali Shapiro, Catherine Hayes, A. L. Major, Gina Balibrera, Dan DiStefano and Dan Frazier, Matt Robison, Amy Cain & the honorable Maya Wild Wild West. For supporting my work and drinking me under the table, I owe you more than I can say.

Thanks to the brilliant Betty Bayer & Susan Henking, whose intellectual and emotional support fortified the foundation on which my world stands. When institutions were not enough, let it be known that Rachel McKibbens gave my work safe haven at the Pink Door Retreat and Andrea/Andrew/Gibby Gibson made sure I got there. My love to all the women and GNC folks I met there. My love, also, to the artists and writers I met at VSC who are in this book, who seeded it.

Because friendship is powerful and love is everything they said it would be, this book would not exist were it not for my living angels, my oldest friends, Marina Jabsky, Marina Litvinskaya, Liza Petrova, Vadim Ledvin, Josh Stewart, Bekah Dinnerstein, Essayan Hart, Hannah Kempf, Jacqui Sands, Jennie Seidewand, Julia Gibson & Kyoko Nakamaru; and, the ones that have sustained my work along the way: Bones Patterson, Karina Vahitova, Alina Pleskova, Sonya Vatomsky, Raena Shirali, Jayson

Smith, Carley Moore, Dia Felix, Sara Jane Stoner, Iemanja Brown, Aricka Foreman, Diane Seuss, Samiya Bashir, Dana Kletter, Angela Watrous, Molly Caldwell, Adjua Gargi Nzinga Greaves, Georgia Sanford, Lisa Del Monte & Tennessee Jones.

My undying love to Stephanie Hopkins & Dawn Lundy Martin for the gorgeous space they carved out for me and for being my family. My undying love to my blood family, my mother and brother.

This book holds Ana Auspitz in deep regard but it breathes because of all my past and present lovers. So, if you're reading this, even if you don't see your name, know that I cherish you.

Coffee House Press began as a small letterpress operation in 1972 and has grown into an internationally renowned nonprofit publisher of literary fiction, essay, poetry, and other work that doesn't fit neatly into genre categories.

Coffee House is both a publisher and an arts organization. Through our *Books in Action* program and publications, we've become interdisciplinary collaborators and incubators for new work and audience experiences. Our vision for the future is one where a publisher is a catalyst and connector.

LITERATURE
is not the same thing as
PUBLISHING

Funder Acknowledgments

Coffee House Press is an internationally renowned independent book publisher and arts nonprofit based in Minneapolis, MN; through its literary publications and *Books in Action* program, Coffee House acts as a catalyst and connector—between authors and readers, ideas and resources, creativity and community, inspiration and action.

Coffee House Press books are made possible through the generous support of grants and donations from corporations, state and federal grant programs, family foundations, and the many individuals who believe in the transformational power of literature. This activity is made possible by the voters of Minnesota through a Minnesota State Arts Board Operating Support grant, thanks to the legislative appropriation from the Arts and Cultural Heritage Fund. Coffee House also receives major operating support from the Amazon Literary Partnership, the Jerome Foundation, McKnight Foundation, Target Foundation, and the National Endowment for the Arts (NEA). To find out more about how NEA grants impact individuals and communities, visit www.arts.gov.

Coffee House Press receives additional support from the Elmer L. & Eleanor J. Andersen Foundation; the David & Mary Anderson Family Foundation; Bookmobile; Fredrikson & Byron, P.A.; Dorsey & Whitney LLP; the Fringe Foundation; Kenneth Koch Literary Estate; the Knight Foundation; the Matching Grant Program Fund of the Minneapolis Foundation; Mr. Pancks' Fund in memory of Graham Kimpton; the Schwab Charitable Fund; Schwegman, Lundberg & Woessner, P.A.; the U.S. Bank Foundation; and VSA Minnesota for the Metropolitan Regional Arts Council.

The Publisher's Circle of Coffee House Press

Publisher's Circle members make significant contributions to Coffee House Press's annual giving campaign. Understanding that a strong financial base is necessary for the press to meet the challenges and opportunities that arise each year, this group plays a crucial part in the success of Coffee House's mission.

Recent Publisher's Circle members include many anonymous donors, Suzanne Allen, Patricia A. Beithon, the E. Thomas Binger & Rebecca Rand Fund of the Minneapolis Foundation, Andrew Brantingham, Robert & Gail Buuck, Dave & Kelli Cloutier, Louise Copeland, Jane Dalrymple-Hollo, Mary Ebert & Paul Stembler, Kaywin Feldman & Jim Lutz, Chris Fischbach & Katie Dublinski, Sally French, Jocelyn Hale & Glenn Miller, the Rehael Fund-Roger Hale/Nor Hall of the Minneapolis Foundation, Randy Hartten & Ron Lotz, Dylan Hicks & Nina Hale, William Hardacker, Randall Heath, Jeffrey Hom, Carl & Heidi Horsch, the Amy L. Hubbard & Geoffrey J. Kehoe Fund, Kenneth & Susan Kahn, Stephen & Isabel Keating, the Kenneth Koch Literary Estate, Cinda Kornblum, Jennifer Kwon Dobbs & Stefan Liess, the Lambert Family Foundation, the Lenfestey Family Foundation, Sarah Lutman & Rob Rudolph, the Carol & Aaron Mack Charitable Fund of the Minneapolis Foundation, George & Olga Mack, Joshua Mack & Ron Warren, Gillian McCain, Malcolm S. McDermid & Katie Windle, Mary & Malcolm McDermid, Sjur Midness & Briar Andresen, Maureen Millea Smith & Daniel Smith, Peter Nelson & Jennifer Swenson, Enrique & Jennifer Olivarez, Alan Polsky, Marc Porter & James Hennessy, Robin Preble, Alexis Scott, Ruth Stricker Dayton, Jeffrey Sugerman & Sarah Schultz, Nan G. & Stephen C. Swid, Kenneth Thorp in memory of Allan Kornblum & Rochelle Ratner, Patricia Tilton, Joanne Von Blon, Stu Wilson & Melissa Barker, Warren D. Woessner & Iris C. Freeman, and Margaret Wurtele.

For more information about the Publisher's Circle and other ways to support Coffee House Press books, authors, and activities, please visit www.coffeehousepress.org/pages/support or contact us at info@coffeehousepress.org.

Gala Mukomolova earned an MFA from the University of Michigan. She is the author of the chapbook *One Above / One Below: Positions & Lamentations* (YesYes Books 2018), and her work has appeared in *PEN America, Poetry, PANK, Vinyl,* and elsewhere. In 2016 Mukomolova won the 92nd Street Y Discovery/Boston Review Poetry Prize.

Without Protection was designed by Bookmobile Design & Digital Publisher Services. Text is set in Warnock Pro.